How to Play
Three Position Football

Pass-Catch-Defend
An Instructional Game for Boys and Girls

The Complete Rules and Regulations Book

Created by

Karl J. Niemiec

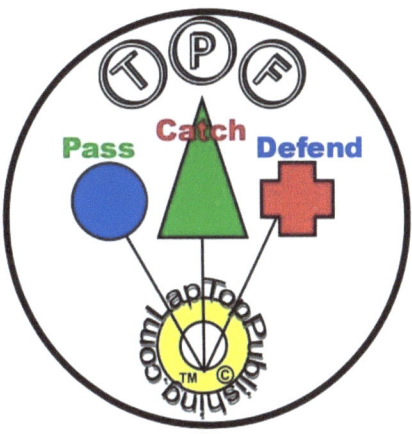

A perfect football game for school curriculum, enrichment programs and fundraising tournaments.

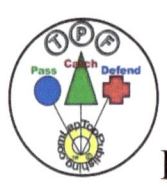 **How to Play Three Position Football**

Copyright © 2011 by Karl J. Niemiec – LapTopPublishing.com

All rights reserved. No part of this book may be reproduced or transmitted in any form or by any means without written permission of the author.

ISBN 978-0-9833663-5-5

LapTopPublishing.com
P.O. Box 3501 Carmel, Indiana 46082
KJN@LapTopPublishing.com

Goals of this Football Game:

The overall goal of this game is to teach players the fundamentals of Leadership, Following Instructions and Self Reliance through the basic elements of organized football.

A secondary goal of TPF, beyond creating paid coaching jobs, is to give teachers and coaches a chance to hone their football mentoring skills. This game is a great opportunity to pass down fundamental elements of football, position techniques and game theories that were gifted to them during their playing days, and will help keep alive the football wisdom from their dads, mentors, teachers and coaches for football-playing generations to come.

*Get your TPF Game Ball
with your name and logo imprinted.*

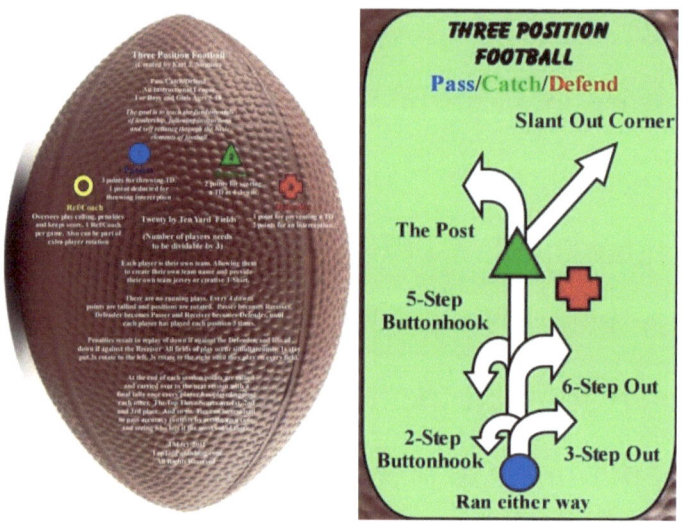

A TPF Game Ball imprint with full rules and route tree can be personalized to fit your organization under an exclusive licensing program with LapTopPublishing.com.

Example would be:
NFL - Three Position Football

To order, please contact LapTopPublishing.com
At: KJN@LapTopPublishing.com

https://www.createspace.com/3733851

Table of Contents

1 – History of the Game 1

2 – Who Can Play TPF? 7

3 – Summary of Rules and Penalties 13

4 – Individual/Combo Teams 17

5 – Three Skilled Positions 21

6 – Who is the Ref? 29

7 – Teaching Basic Skills 31

8 – Basic Six Play Route Tree 35

9 – Pass-Catch-Defend Scoring 37

10 – Rotate Every Four Downs 39

11 – Tournament Structure 41

12 - Size of Football and Field 45

13 - Divide Players by Three 47

Other Games by Karl J. Niemiec 51

1 – History of the Game

It has been said that Three Position Football brings the Madden NFL Video Games to life, because kids have a choice of what plays to pick, get to tweak them a little bit, and make them their own.

Three Position Football has been played in most backyards since the beginning of football. What does it take to play? At least Three Players, enough space and a football. This is true to how I developed this game into a fun curriculum and fundraising tournament.

The summer that I turned 12 years old, just a skinny kid no-bigger than four-two or three at a push, my next oldest brother Ben was 13 ½ years old and already much bigger than I was back then.

It was that summer my mother remarried to one of the coaches in our football league in Farmington, Michigan on the 4th of July, the very day my championship baseball team was to play in a tournament representing our league in Canada. I didn't realize it at the time, but this was both one of the best things to ever happen to me, and the highlight of my sports career. For moving gave me a perspective in life that I surely wouldn't ever of had otherwise, one of living in the country, raising horses, pitching manure, bailing hay and going to a small school where everyone knew each other. But better yet, it's where I learned how to type and more so I learned the meaning of being a good person. To this day, most of everything I know how to do came from living in Jonesville, Michigan. My mother is buried there, just off US 12 and for those memories and those life lessons, Jonesville will always be in my heart.

As it turned out, my mother's new husband had two children, John and Joanne. John was around 6 months older than I and played in the same football and baseball bracket as I. My oldest brother, Fred, coached some of my football teams, whereas John's father coached his teams. And that's apparently how my mother and George came to know each other.

The interesting thing was, John was not in my grade in school, he was in my brother Ben's grade, and was just a little more than 6 months or so younger than Ben. So he fit right in the middle of us both.

One day, shortly after the wedding, Mom and George up and moved us out to that great town at the boarder of Michigan and Ohio - population hovering around 2000 people, and planted us on a 40 acre farm, with horses, manure and hay - though no one else in the immediate area but us three boys to play sports with.

So we started to play an untitled version of football at the time, that I now call Three Position Football - Pass, Catch and Defend. The title I later developed through my memories of this game before pitching the game

How to play Three Position Football

to a Parks and Recreation Manager in Studio City, California as a fall sports program, where I took my son, Vaughn James to play in the sand. It was there during my presentation I began to develop these childhood memories of playing football with my brothers into a teachable format and designed the tournament structure for boys and girls of all ages.

In looking back at playing this game with my brothers, I learned, even though I was much smaller than my brothers, that I had my fair opportunity to keep up with them because of how Three Position Football is inherently structured.

Because I could throw, and I could defend, and I could catch, it didn't matter that they were so much bigger, better skilled and older than I. I had just as much chance of scoring and winning as they did because of the point structure evened the playing field. And that success and chance of winning every time we played stuck in my head and heart.

The fond memory of those days in the fall and later in the snow of playing that game wedged itself into my happy-zone and it festered over many years until I finally had a reason to write it down and create a full blown tournament and school curriculum based on that very game we played out on the front lawn of our farmhouse.

And this is the very football game that came out of playing it according to my memories of those days back in the late 1960's. The differences are: the enhanced scoring structure, the expanded tournament structure, the added Ref/Coach/Player, the option of multiple sizes of balls and fields,

Karl J. Niemiec

the ability to create coaching jobs, the developing of afterschool programs, the fund raising tournaments at all sports levels, and the giving rise to an easy to construct school football curriculum.

Everyone who has seen, heard or played TPF immediately have become hooked on the simplicity of the game, yet the complexity of its potential to be played anywhere anytime as long as there are three players or the ability to use the forth as a Ref/Coach/Player rotation.

This is how Three Position Football came to be structured into this tournament game. A game I hope you'll all find as fun and educational as did I when I first strapped on my tennis shoes and played the game with my brothers overlooking US 12, halfway between Detroit and Chicago in 1968.

Read Testimonials:

Thank you, Karl for introducing TPF to LDF. The Children had a fantastic time. You were correct; the game is designed for everyone no matter the size, the gender, or age of the players. After we got started what a joy to see all the children having so much fun! Thanks again for LapTopPublishing.com's support of the Lillian Davis Foundation 2011 Summer Enrichment Camp. Your Friend, LaMarr Davis, President

Karl, I just saw the video tonight on YouTube and I love it! I would like to download this video on our website and also show it in our orientation Saturday. Marion Robinson LDF

Videos of:

Lillian Davis Foundation playing TPF and commentary from John Zangrilli, Wellness Instructor at Woodbrook Elementary School – Carmel, Indiana (2nd - 5th Grades) and Coach of Zionsville, IN Varsity Baseball Team.

Watch At: http://laptoppublishing.com/ThreePositionFootball.html

How to play Three Position Football

In 1972, Ben played on the now nationally famous State Champion high school team, Fordson Tractors - featured on "All American Muslims."

The Jonesville Wild Bunch
Ben, John and Karl

2 – Who Can Play TPF?

This is an instructional football game intended for boys and girls of all ages and physical/social skillsets. And that is part of the natural beauty of this particular football game structure. Because it is intended to be instructional and each player is their own team, there is no need to leave any player willing to play out of this game, regardless of gender or skillset. Kids who have never played in recess games or played organized football can reach out and enjoy the fundamentals of football for the first time because each player only represents him/herself

One of the most attractive aspects of this game is that every player on the field plays in every down and has an opportunity to touch the ball on every play, either to pass it, catch it, defend it, or as an added Ref/Coach/Player place the football and keep the individual scores.

Because of the desired lack of contact in this game, girls can safely play the game with the boys or play within their own tournaments.

LEVELS OF PLAY

Grade School:

- Gym Curriculum.
- After School Enrichment Programs
- School Fundraising Tournaments
- Intramural District Tournaments
- Beginning Skill Training Programs

Junior High:

- After School Enrichment Programs
- School Fundraising Tournaments
- Intramural District Tournaments
- Advance Skill Training Programs

High School:

- After School Enrichment Programs
- School Fundraising Tournaments
- Extramural District Tournaments
- Team Skill Training Programs

How to play Three Position Football

Special Needs Programs:

- After School Enrichment Programs
- School Fundraising Tournaments
- Intramural District Tournaments
- Team Skill Training Programs

Church Organizations:

- Gym Curriculum
- After School Enrichment Programs
- Fundraising Tournaments
- Intramural Church Tournaments
- Beginning Skill Training Programs

YMCA, Sport Parks, Athletic-Centers:

- Team Sponsored Tournaments
- Advance Private Training Programs
- Mixed Gender-Individual Player-Teams
- Intramural Park/YMCA Tournaments
- Beginning Skill Training Programs

Karl J. Niemiec

NCAA - University and Junior College:

- Competition between Fraternities
- Competition between Sororities
- Cheerleaders Tournament Fundraising
- Educational Prize Grant Money

Restaurants and Bar Leagues:

- Moral building Summer/Fall events
- Competition between Bars/Restaurants
- Charity Tournament Fundraising
- Prize Money
- Intramural Chain Restaurants from Hooters to McDonald's
- Four Star Hotels
- Vegas Night Clubs

USA Football Leagues:

- Extramural Travel Teams of all ages
- Local and National Individual Tournaments
- Skill Training Leagues – Players and Coaches

How to play Three Position Football

Arena - Canadian- NFL Leagues:

- Cheerleader Tournament Fundraising
- Retired NFL Tournament fundraising
- TV Tournament Programming.
  NFL Films or independently

This is just some of the ways this game can fit into existing sports programs that are looking for something new and a simpler way to organize their football activates that include both boys and girls.

Every town, city, county and state has their own available space and sports budget, both private and state funded. So the different types of sport-organizations that can easily put this kind of Football Program together are fundamentally endless. Because the individual team scoring structure allows for not-relying on putting together 5-11 player teams. The amount of entry fees and basic gym class involvement can greatly increased because of the multiple games taking place, and the different age levels of boys and girls in both tournaments and school curriculums.

This can lead to multiple levels of advertisements and possible marketing of video to local and national TV as well as training videos for individual players looking to accumulate video on their skills or develop training video as sport trainers and coaches.

3 – Summary of Rules and Penalties

The number of game/tournament-players works best when they are dividable by 3 player/teams. But often there will be an unavoidable odd number of players. In which case the odd number player can start as a Ref/Coach/Player and rotated into the playing field in a four player field.

As stated in Chapter 12, the basic field size is Twenty by Ten Yard Fields but can be marked by cones to fit existing spaces or the skill levels of the players. As is the case with the ball size, make of ball and hardness.

Standard pass penalty rules result in replay of down if against the Defender, and loss of down if against the Receiver.

One Ref/Coach per game encourages viewing parents/classmates to participate because all the fields of play occur simultaneously. This also allows for that occasional added fourth player into the field of rotation when necessary because of an odd number of players.

There are no running plays. And Receiver is down where he/she catches the ball. This evens the playing field speed wise and helps to eliminate injuries due to attempting to stop the Receiver from moving the ball forward on foot. This also allows for continues passing plays to move the ball towards scoring.

And every 4 downs, points are tallied by the Ref/Coach or players themselves and positions are rotated. Passer becomes Receiver, Defender becomes Passer and Receiver becomes Defender, until each player has played each position 3 times.

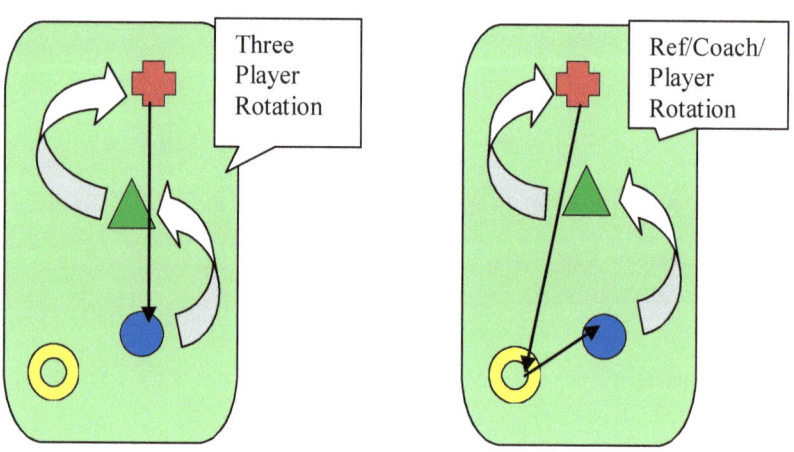

At the end of each session points are then tallied and either tracked on a scoreboard or on individual scorecards kept by the players. These scores should be marked down or verified by the Ref/Coach/Player if possible. There is an honor system of keeping one's own score such that exists in golf without the Mulligans.

When all three (four if there's a Ref/Player) positions are played three times on all the fields of play and every player has played against each other, the *Top Three Scores* are 1st 2nd and 3rd places. And so on. Ties can be resolved in a pass accuracy contests by setting up a cone and

How to play Three Position Football

seeing who hits it the most out of three. The amount of turns at each position can be adjusted as needed for any given situation or rotation can be suspended all together to fit curriculum time allotment needs.

If so desired the top final three scorers or any number of top scores can play one last round. This of course is flexible per the organizations needs and time allotments. But can add a whole new level of playoff excitement to the tournament.

At 10, my son Vaughn James Niemiec helped teach Three Position Football to The Lillian Davis Foundation in Indianapolis, Indiana.

4 – Individual/Combo Teams

As designed, each player is their own team. Allowing them to create their own team name and provide their own team jersey or creative T-Shirt.

Karl J. Niemiec

T-Shirts can also display individual sponsors such as the shirts in these photos sponsored by LapTopPublishing.com.

These Sponsored T-Shirts can be for individual players or for the whole tournaments. Or can be a combo of sponsors, sponsoring the whole TPF program, fraternity, cheerleaders, charity. Or just bought or made up into the coolest/flashiest/sexiest individual team T-Shirt by each individual team player. This is all depending on who is organizing the tournament, from Hooters to Church leagues, and what their overall goals are.

The options here for add-placements and individual expression is endless and each tournament as stated will naturally need to create their own set of T-Shirt rules and guidelines per that tournament image.

Another cool aspect of this football game is that, much like bowling leagues, groups can enter these games as sponsored teams but each individual player's score is tracked through the tournament, and would be his personal score based on his/her own skillset and effort, even though they are all wearing the same team shirts sponsored by whoever funded their participation in the tournament.

As far as community and school involvement, this football game is a perfect way for school coaching staffs to monitor the skillset of all players moving through their school system so that by the time they have reached JV and Varsity Football Programs, the coaches already have a tractable and verifiable written document, and often video showing the skillsets of each player moving into their football program.

How to play Three Position Football

A tracking record of winning and playing within this kind of tournament can also be used by the players as part of their attempts to move on to higher football levels as they grow up within a sports system.

5 – Three Skilled Positions

While developing a Three Position Football program coaches will get to work with each player individually as he/she moves from field to field during the course of play. Even when played all at once and there's ten to twenty games taking place, it's easy to watch individual players and there's ample time to take a moment to make subtle adjustments to the player's fundamental football technique. A coach/teacher can also take a moment to speak to the whole playing field if he/she needs to either remind all players to abide by a basic rule or how to hone basic skills by showing an example of good technique verses bad technique in Passing, Receiving or Defending a play. These windows of teaching opportunities will happen naturally as the game progresses. And coaches will have ample time to note the different levels of agility of the players

With the help of using the basic *Pass Route Tree* (ran both ways) provided in this book the Passer learns leadership and how to call the correct play needed to move the ball systematically down the field to score.

Karl J. Niemiec

With good coaching from those running the program he/she learns the basic skills of how to hold the ball correctly, develop better footwork, and how to throw the ball with the proper velocity to a timed and accurate area so that only the Receiver can catch it. Due to the limited space and the one pass route per play the Passer is taught to time his throws to arrive to the designed end play spot, and be thrown in a place where the Receiver can catch it in bounds. At times he'll have to choose to not throw the ball at all, throw it away to keep from throwing an obvious interception, or choose to risk the throw in trusting that his Receiver will adjust to the ball or prevent an interception himself. This is part of the leadership quality that will develop while playing this game, being able to recognized and trust his/her own opinion of the skillsets between each Receiver/Defender he/she comes in contact with.

Even if a player is destined to eventually play offensive or defensive line because of size and/or speed in whatever full contact league they would eventually play in, getting a first chance to play the Passer consistently in this football game will not only be a unique experience it will be a highly beneficial opportunity to hone their own leadership skills; as well as getting a better overall grasp of the position they are trying to protect or crush in full contact football.

This part of the skillset of where and when to throw the football that only the Receiver has a chance to catch it - should/can - be taught continuously by the instructor or Ref/Coach who is running that particular field or by a coach who is running the entire game or tournament.

How to play Three Position Football

Regardless of where the Passer's skillset begins each player's technique will grow significantly because of the simple reason of repetition and having the opportunity to throw the ball and follow the examples by Ref/Coaches and the other players they play against. This is part of the value of having a Ref/Coach overseeing the field - to help players work on their techniques in all three skill aspects of the game.

Learning how to call plays from the reversible selected plays in the provided route tree, or in many cases, plays designed by specific coaches who are using this game as part of their team training sessions, is part of the leadership and confidence building aspects of this game and also helps hone the skill of remembering the play names by all the players, regardless of what position those players end up playing during regular organized scheduled football practice and games.

Receivers learn how to run and follow precise diagramed directions, either the pass routes designed within the TPF game or by the coaches who use this game for skillset training purposes for his school, intramural play or on traveling teams, etc.

In TPF the Receiver gets one defined route to run, and once that designated route is over he/she cannot run around the field haphazardly to get open. So, it becomes instinctive to look for, to be ready to catch and to expect the ball to be thrown to a designed catchable spot.

Also, the Receiver is down where he catches the ball. This extends the amount of plays called, helps prevent collisions, discourages rough play, limits sports related concussions and promotes keeping one's hands off the other player, both offensively and defensively.

Since the play is over once the called route has been run, it is in part the other players' and/or the Ref/Coach to make sure this strict rule is followed on every pass play so that the game doesn't lose its focused and become a free-for-all on pass patterns, ultimately wasting playing time. Of course, in a real football game extended pass plays are common, taught and expected. But for this training/playing experience we are encouraging players to abide by this single pass route rule. Regardless, making up plays during routes should be discouraged to keep the game moving forward in an organized manner of play, unless there is an adjustment made universally throughout the tournament by those organizing that particular game; including backyard play.

What's also significantly cool about this game is that players can bring in their own pass routes, or full route trees, that they have learned from other team action, or routes that were taught by their dad's or big brothers or learned when playing football in the street with the neighborhood kids.

A way to organize this added play use is to have these plays submitted, fully diagramed and named to the tournament leaders before play begins so that everyone playing the game is aware of them and knows what the designed route is ahead of time.

In the big picture of the game, beyond inherent and learned catching skills, what matters most is that players who run pass patterns aspire to run the routes as drawn so that they are where they are supposed to be when the ball gets there, since timed pass/routes are the very backbones of this game.

Part of this pass running talent is developing the art of deception in fooling the Defender to commit himself to defend what he/she perceives the pass route to be. This is an art form that is both inherent and taught and can mean the difference of overcoming speed and size between the Receiver and Defender. With less experienced players, learning how to use size advantages, going up over the head of the Defender for the ball, or using inherent speed and quickness to get to the ball first, is a learned skill that most new players can make adjustments to if taught how to recognize them in themselves, and then to use them correctly.

Because penalties are called on both the offence and defense, in running pass patterns the Receiver is taught not to push off on the Defender because of offensive interference. He/she is also taught how to avoid being rerouted by the Defender to stay within the strict called routes. He will learn how to expect the ball thrown to a designated spot that only the Receiver can get to, and to be ready to catch it when he/she turns to the ball. The Receiver is also taught how to adjust to the ball thrown to an open area within the route. These kinds of skill training techniques depend on the level of coaching and learning from fellow players, plus the level of skillset each Receiver brings to his/her game. A learning curve will begin from the first field of play and it will be an obvious arc of development in all players regardless of the basic skillset brought into the game.

As in most ball-sports, all catching the ball skills include losing the fear of being hit in the face with the ball. This is a learning process of hand-eye coordination, and is based on individual successes and confidence levels development and reinforced within each set of downs. A significant noticeable growth pattern will occur during each game and tournament based on the level of trust of one's own natural talents combined with encouragement from coaches and fellow players. Choosing and using the right type of ball, soft or hard, big or small, for the skillset level of the overall players comes in play here and of course will often depend on the budget and availably of buying different types of balls.

Also, at times a Receiver will have to defend the ball from being taken away by the Defender. This too, is a learned skill without committing interference or pushing off. The skillset of this technique will vary and will come in play with the growth of trust between Receiver and Passer as to when to hold or throw the ball into tight coverage. The bigger and stronger the Receiver the more chances the Passer may take in forcing the ball into the tight coverage. Understanding the skillset of the Defender obviously comes into play here and is part of the player growth on both the Passer's and Receiver's part. When a Ref/Coach/Player is involved this may be discussed between them to include everyone in the huddle. This will enhance communication skills amongst players. Watching NCAA and NFL games and discussing these kind of coverage between

How to play Three Position Football

coaches, dads and players is part of the overall football experience, and having a game like this that all kids/players can grasps helps the understanding and enjoyment of the NCAA and NFL experience, possibly inspiring whole new generations of TV viewing fans who wouldn't otherwise grasp the complexity of the game.

Defender: Learns how to be self reliant on his defensive skills. Because there is no running after the catch, the Defender must develop a sense of knowing how to decipher what type (the depth) of play the Passer will call in any given passing down in light of how many yards the Receiver needs covered to score points. Very much like any defensive coordinator would do in calling defensive plays for a team.

Of course defending the ball, keeping the Receiver from catching it, is a primary talent developed by the Defender, and will be enhanced by the directions of Coaches and Parent/Refs as the games progress. But another big part of playing-the-ball while keeping hands off the Receiver is being able to take the ball away to gain more points. Therefore, a significant portion of training a Defender in this game is spent on timing and catching the ball - as well as the ability to reach in and make the Receiver drop it without creating a foul.

Since speed and agility levels will vary from player to player, and the playing this size of field is designed for one pass pattern per play only, a Defender needs to develop an inner process to foresee what the Passer is planning before the play commences and needs to be able to adjust to the fakes and deception of skilled Receivers trying to make the Defender commit to defending the wrong portion of the playing field.

This ability to react with an instinctive move to position oneself in the right place at the right time is part of the defending skillset and something all Defenders will quickly develop while playing TPF, regardless of where they are skillset wise when they start to play.

Players who would not normally get a chance to play Defender will benefit greatly in using this game as an agility builder, learning to read the natural movements of the Passer and growing a sense of moving to the ball at all times. Overall, there are no limits to Three Position Football for giving kids who don't normally get a chance to play the skilled positions to shine on the football field and feel the exhilaration of touching the ball on every play. Not only will this game build all basic agility skills, strengthen overall body functions, it will enhance the enjoyment and understanding of the game for everyone involved, especially those kids who have never played the game, or watched the game, beyond sitting on the sidelines and watching their peers play at recess.

6 – Who is the Ref?

 Ref/Coach/Player:

One of the cool aspects of TPF tournament structure is the constant flexibility of the fourth Ref/Coach/Player position on the field. Traditionally played in the backyard, the three players - Passer, Receiver, and Defender - would oversee their own scores and call their own fouls as based on the basic rules of touch football. Scores would be called out after each play and added to the totals of each player so that all players involved on that field of play are in total agreement of what the current scores are, at all times. As in any game, an accurate account of scores is mandatory. But with an added Ref/Coach/ Player, or such as a participating parent, wellness instructor or football coach, this person would be included in every playing field as need/available to oversee scoring and fouls. It is best to use Ref/Coaches in most large tournament games; however using Ref/Coach/Players is completely adequate to fulfill the needs of overseeing the game on a large scale. This added leadership position gives young players a sense of responsibility of making important and decisive sportsmanship related calls, plus join other huddles.

Also, keeping score on multiple levels gives young players a need to understand and utilize basic math skills. Again, this allows all players on the field to participate in continuous football related skills on every down.

7 – Teaching Basic Skills

With Three Position Football there is plenty of room to exercise one's skills in teaching the fundamentals of football in both a broad approach and single player situation during the course of play.

Having presented that concept, in many cases, the first portion of a Gym Class or Football Practice can be spent recapping the skillset learned from previous games or to go over the basic skills needed to start playing Three Position Football.

Connecting individually with the players so they all get a chance to understand the Basic 6 Play Route Tree is important so that everyone is on the same page in knowing they can be run either way, and the Passer doesn't have to take the time to remind or instruct the Receiver of what route he is calling beyond showing him/her on the included Route Tree Diagram in this book. Added plays are entirely up to the person running the tournament and of course should be submitted for use by all players in any given tournament.

Confusion of pass routes will inadvertently happen but will diminish as the game progresses when each player not only becomes Passer but the Receiver and Defender. This is why it's encouraged to have the Route Tree Diagram available for the Passer to call plays from so he can actually point and show the pass pattern he is calling and to make sure he's using the right name in calling the pass. In between plays the Ref/Coach/Player can hold this Route Tree Diagram to help keep things moving forward smoothly and this will be part of his involvement of the game on every play. This diagram if laminated can be used as a hard backing surface to write on individual score cards if used.

This is also why LapTopPublishing.com offers personalized monogrammed Game Balls that include not only the basic rules of TPF but the 6 Play Route Tree Diagram. So they can be held and read from inside the huddle.

As in any game of football, it is encouraged to have a basic warm-up and skill practice session before beginning to play TPF. This encourages players to stretch and perform basic exercises to help keep them limber and in shape. If basic throwing, running, defending route skills are worked on, this lends for even more heart rate enhancements for even the most sedimentary players as they learn the positions. This includes Defender's agility calisthenics to move backward and sideways with the movement of the ball.

How to play Three Position Football

When coaches, or tournament organizations, are playing against players outside of their facilities, whether it's any school, parks, restaurants or professional levels, the skillset is often a reflection upon the coach who is training and teaching the players the game of football.

So TPF is a great working tool for Coaches to showcase their football teaching skills and can be used as a platform to enhance their careers in coaching or teaching sports to both young and adult players. As in any skill position of football, Coaching is as important as any of the others. And since TPF is a very hands on individual driven interactive game, all Coaches can take advantage of building their resumes by organizing and promoting the skillsets they bring to this football game.

8 – Basic Six Play Route Tree

Though the diagram below only shows six patterns, each pattern can be reversed to run to the other side of the playing field and/or adjusted by multiple lengths to add even more plays to the Route Tree.

There is no reason that existing plays from different levels of games, schools, coaches and or individual players can't be inserted into this game to give the players a sense of ownership or to fulfill training requirements for particular groups playing TPF.

Keep in mind that this game is designed as not only a very fun way to teach and play football it is designed to be a teaching tool of the basic football fundamentals based on pass plays and utilizing the three skills of passing, catching and defending to teach leadership, following directions and self reliance.

I've provided a basic Route Tree, but if you Google "Route Tree" you will find many Route Tree Diagrams to work with to design your own plays and Route Trees.

As stated before, because there are no running plays and the Receiver is down after the catch, part of skillset of this game for the Passer is to design plays that will systematically move the ball across the goal line to gain points. Obviously, completing all four pass attempts doesn't equate to points unless the Receiver catches the ball across the goal line. So the Passer must design his play calling not only to fool the Defender but also to move the ball across the goal line, whether it takes one pass or all four. Therefore, not to throw a touchdown gives the Defender a point even if the Receiver catches all four passes. So obviously part of the skillset of the Receiver is not to let the Defender put him/her off running their routes that would lead them to points, and part of the Defender's skillset is to keep the Receiver from running his/her routes without causing a interference penalty. Regardless at the end of each four down set, at least one point is awarded to a player.

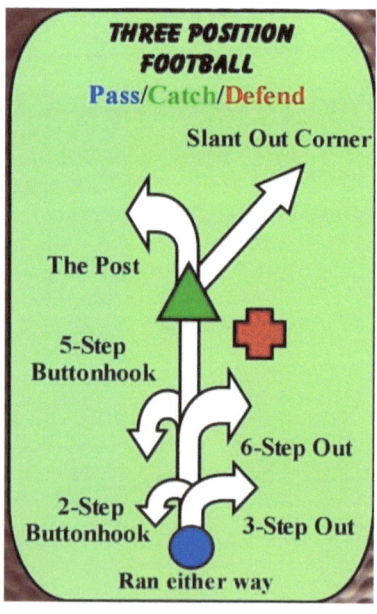

9 – Pass-Catch-Defend Scoring

Keeping score is up to the TPF organizer. Sometimes keeping score isn't possible or necessary to play the game, as in some time limited school gym curriculum. But the basic scoring if used goes as follows:

Passer:

3 points for throwing a TD
1 point deducted for
throwing an interception

Receiver:

2 points for scoring a TD
Note: No points are deducted from Receiver if an interception is thrown, just loss of ball possession, and Players rotate positions

Defender:

1 point for preventing a TD
2 points for catching an interception
Note: One or the other, not both.

10 – Rotate Every Four Downs

Every four downs points are tallied and positions are rotated. Passer becomes Receiver, Defender becomes Passer and Receiver becomes Defender, until each player has played each position three times.

Full player scoreboards can be used to keep score or be kept individually on players' scorecards, or by the Ref/Coach/Player who also oversees play calling and penalties.

As stated in the Summery of Rules chapter, penalties result in replay of down if against the Defender, and loss of down if against the Receiver.

One Ref/Coach/Player per game encourages viewing parents/classmates to participate because all the fields of play occur simultaneously. This also allows for adding a fourth player into the rotation if necessary and solving an odd number of players so that no one gets turned away.

Karl J. Niemiec

11 – Tournament Structure

As at any football level of play, from backyard, little league, high school, NCAA and the NFL, playing football is a continuous learning process. I'm amazed at how many times we hear NFL coaches and football analyst argue the learning process of players entering the NFL and the difference of speed between NCAA and the NFL. You would think that the player had never played the game before. And often the analyst express amazement at how fast a rookie does well in the NFL. This can be explained in the increase in complexity of the playbook and condensing of the skillset level of players which include intelligence, speed, agility and overall strength.

This is also true with TPF in part due to available playing space, number of players participating, as well as the skillset levels of the overall program. Therefore, a TPF organizer should be flexible in how their tournament is structured to fit the given skillset of participating players. Not only in size of field, but size of ball, whether or not girls and boys play together, and even if the Receiver should be allowed to advance the ball after a catch. In the big picture of this football game, it is completely up to the organizers to decide how the basic rules of this Three Position Football structure fits into their world of play. But once it's decided as to what fits a given playing space, it should stay consistent throughout the tournament so everyone plays the same game within the same rules. If during play a basic fundamental rule needs tweaked then it should be announce throughout the tournament so everyone knows.

For this book, the basic player/team rotation goes as follows:

- Player #1 stays put and plays all football sessions on the same playing field. ⊗
- Player #2 would shift left. ⟵
- Player #3 would shift right. ⟶
- Ref/Coach/Player would play twice in 1st field then shift right.
- Until Players #2, #3 and RCFs have played on all playing fields and/or all players have played the same amount of downs.
- Once all players have played each other, the tournament ends and the player with the highest score wins.
- For additional play, a preselected number of the highest scoring players can move on to the next level.
- They can either bring their scores with them, or start from zero points and play a shorter form of the tournament.
- The number of levels of play can be determined at the beginning of each tournament depending on how much time each session has, how many playing days are available and how many players are involved. Eliminated players can Coach/Ref to stay active.

How to play Three Position Football

12 - Size of Football and Field

When organizing this game, every available playing space, indoors or outdoors, in each given tournament will be different. But in this book, the basic field space is Ten by Twenty Yard Fields, and even smaller for very young players.

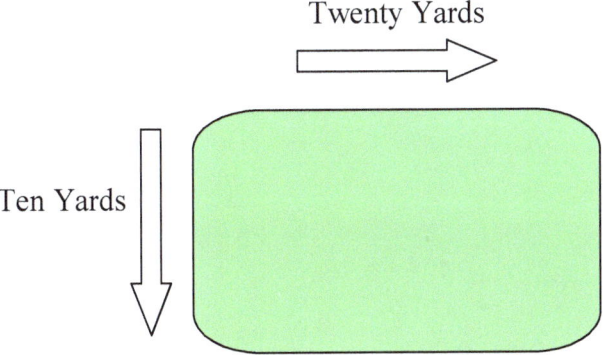

And of course the field can be lengthened and widen to fit the skillset level of the players or available space for the appropriate tournament. Part of this reasoning is taking into account the average distance – the ability to throw accurately for the overall participating players. Proper field-sizes can be averaged with simple throwing distance exercises.

Karl J. Niemiec

13 - Divide Players by Three

For obvious reasons the player count works best if divided by three, hence the name Three Position Football. However, as stated in previous chapters, a fourth player can be added to the position rotation by allowing one of the players on that designated field to become a Ref/Coach/Player and be involved in score keeping, penalty calling and play verification. This allows for flexibility in all given situations to insure no player wanting to play, or in some cases as in school curriculums having to play, is left out from participating on every single down.

As stated, having only three players to play football with back in the day in Jonesville, Michigan was the notion in which this game came from and is a very realistic number of players to fulfill all needs of training in the basic three skilled positions that encourages a no contact game. Teaching the Defender to keep his hands off the Receiver and also the Receiver to not push off on the Defender are skills all players need to develop as they prefect these two positions. Keeping one's hands to themselves isn't a bad overall life lesson in the big picture of everyday things.

Karl J. Niemiec

Not having a rusher or blocker knocks down the amount of body contact, and teaching noncontact pass coverage helps eliminate head injuries.

John - Ben – Karl in 1968

This game is dedicated to being brothers.

About the Author

Karl J. Niemiec now lives in Carmel, Indiana with his three sons, daughter and wife. His love for the game inspired him to create TPF in hope that everyone will have a chance to play, coach and learn from it - regardless of their social-background, gender or skillset.

Other Games by Karl J. Niemiec

Paperback and Kindle Books
https://www.createspace.com/3716137

DVD - Instant Rental
https://www.createspace.com/245933

Available through LapTopPublishing.com

https://www.amazon.com/author/karljniemiec-laptoppublishin

https://www.createspace.com/3733851

TPF - GAME DAY ROUTE TREE

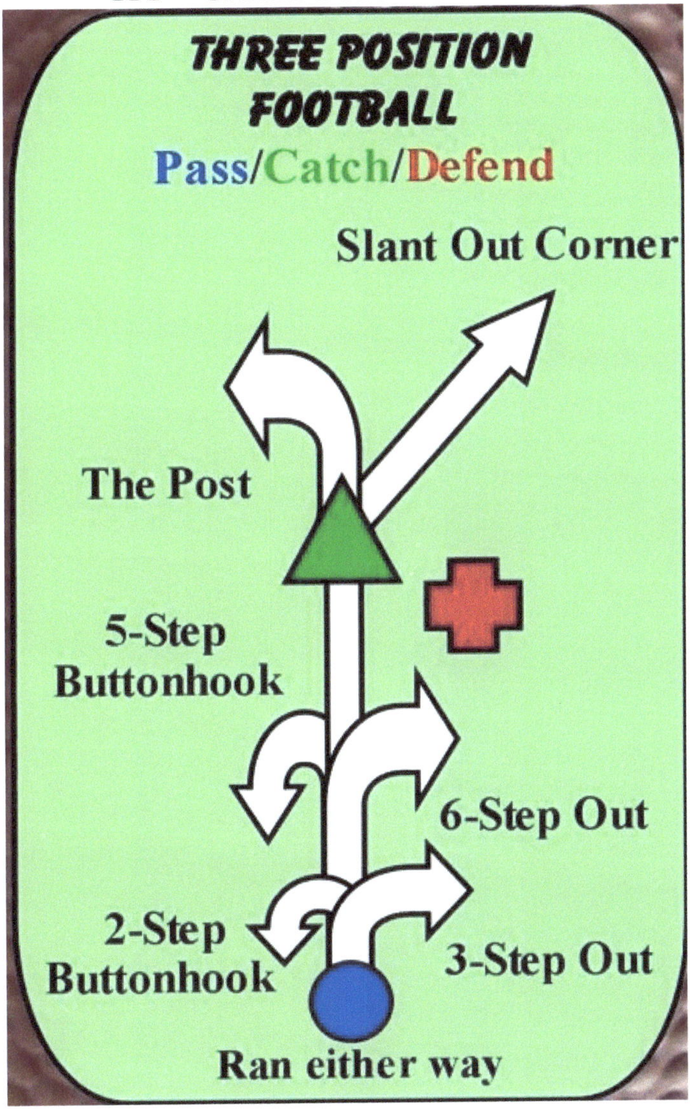

THREE POSITION FOOTBALL
Pass/Catch/Defend

- Slant Out Corner
- The Post
- 5-Step Buttonhook
- 6-Step Out
- 2-Step Buttonhook
- 3-Step Out
- Ran either way

© All Rights Reserved - LapTopPublishing.com

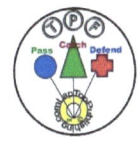

www.ingramcontent.com/pod-product-compliance
Lightning Source LLC
Chambersburg PA
CBHW042335150426
43194CB00005B/169